A study companion to

The income approach to property valuation

A study companion to

The income approach to property valuation

David Mackmin

First published in 1983 by the Department of Land Management and Development as No. 2 in their student guide series on Appraisal ISBN 0 7049 0829 8.
Second edition published by Routledge 1990
11 New Fetter Lane, London, EC4P 4EE
29 West 35th Street, New York, NY 10001

Camera-ready material by Sonning Business Services, Reading.

Printed and bound in Great Britain by
Biddles Ltd, Guildford and King's Lynn

British Library Cataloguing in Publication Data

Mackmin, David, 1944-
A study companion to the income approach to property valuation - 2nd ed.
1. Great Britain. Investment. Real property. Valuation I. Title II. Baum, Andrew, 1953-. Income approach to property valuation - 3rd ed.
332.63240941

ISBN 0-415-04759-5

Contents

Preface

There is nothing mathematically or conceptually difficult in *The Income Approach to Property Valuation** yet many students will take 12 to 18 months to cover the ground. One reason for this is that a lecturer can only cover a certain amount of material in an hour and many lecturers still believe that such material must be transferred by word of mouth. The result is an unnecessary extension of the time scale.

I knew I could not afford such an extended course for the Reading M.Phil. in Land Management. Indeed to extend the course would be an affront to the intellectual ability of postgraduates. A study companion seemed the logical conclusion and it has allowed most of the material to be covered in ten weeks. Having prepared the companion I felt that it could benefit many other valuation students and would help them to measure their own understanding of the subject.

This study companion is closely related to the main text and has itself sufficient text to help the student to progress rapidly and smoothly to an early holistic appreciation of Income Property Valuation. It is therefore more than a series of questions and answers.

D.H. Mackmin
Reading 1983

* By Andrew Baum and David Mackmin published by Routledge

Preface to second edition

The second edition has been revised in parallel with the third edition of *The Income Approach to Property Valuation*. In revising the companion I have extended the questions on theory and expanded the explanations given in the answers section. The questions are worded in such a way as to guide readers to produce consistent responses. Where readers' solutions disagree with my own they should check carefully to see if they have committed an error in principle for, in the real world of property, valuers rarely produce identical solutions to any given problem.

Having understood the principles, readers should be in a position to gauge with care their ability to undertake property investment valuations in practice where there are no answers, just logically argued professional opinions supported as fully as possible with market evidence.

David Mackmin BSc. MSc. FRICS.
Reading 1990

Chapter one

Valuation mathematics

The aim of these questions is to help the student of valuation find out what he or she does or does not know about the basic mathematics used by investment analysts, investment appraisers and property valuers. The mathematics is common to all forms of investment. Answers can be inserted in the spaces provided. If the answer is wrong then the point should be checked in *The Income Approach to Property Valuation* before proceeding.

Question numbers refer to relevant chapters in the third edition of *The Income Approach to Property Valuation* by Andrew Baum and David Mackmin published by Routledge. A set of standard valuation tables and a calculator will be needed.

1.1   What is the interest on £500 at 8% for one year?

£ _____40.00_____

When money is loaned or borrowed, interest is received or has to be paid at a given rate per cent on the capital or principal (5% = £5 on £100). Interest is a compensation for the loss of liquidity - it is the amount a lender requires for waiting for the use of his capital.

1.2   How much interest would be received after one year on a loan of £2,500 at 9% per annum?   £ __225.00__

If £2,500 is borrowed for one year at 9% per annum, how much interest would have to be paid?   £ __225.00__

1.3   The total amount of interest paid depends on the amount of capital borrowed, the rate of interest and the length of time. Check this relationship by completing the following table.

Principal £	Rate of Interest % p.a.	Time (Years)	Interest £
600	5	1	30
1,000	9	1	90
2,000	20	1	400
57.50	14	1	8.05

1.4 If £5,000 is borrowed on the terms set out below in (a), (b), (c), would the same amount of interest be paid in each case?

Yes/No

What is the total amount of interest in each case?

a) Interest payable annually at the end of each year calculated at the rate of 9%. £ _450_

b) Interest payable after 6 months and 12 months calculated at the rate of 4½% per half year. £ _450_

c) Interest payable at the end of each month calculated at the rate of 0.75% per month. £ _450_

The problem is that different lenders offer different terms. To compare alternatives one needs to find the effective rate of interest. By law, certain lenders must quote a specific type of effective rate known as the Annual Percentage Rate. The APR takes into account all charges in addition to interest such as arrangement fees, ad valorem taxes, etc. APR as such is not used by valuation surveyors but a valuer needs to know in each case whether the rates of interest are 'nominal' or 'effective'.

1.5 Given an annual nominal rate of 12% calculate the effective rate per annum when interest is due (a) monthly, (b) quarterly, (c) half yearly. Remember that in the formula for compound interest 'i' is now the interest rate per period and 'n' is the total number of interest earning periods.

If money is borrowed or loaned for longer than a year the terms of the agreement will require interest to be paid at fixed points during the loan period or interest can be 'rolled up' and paid in full at the end of the loan period.

NOTE. In the case of 'savings' a saver can receive interest at fixed points in time and withdraw interest for spending or interest can be left as a credit, in which case the account accumulates. The term Compound Annual Rate CAR may be used in this context.

1.6 Mr. X deposits £100 in a building society investment account earning interest at 10% p.a. effective. Complete this table to show

how much he will have in 5 years' time.

Start of year	Principal at start of each year £	Interest at 10% p.a. at end of year
1	100	*19*
2	*110*	*11*
3	*121*	
4		
5		

1.7 Calculate the equivalent salary in 3 years' time of a trainee surveyor now earning £10,000 per annum, assuming that the rate of salary inflation is 12% p.a.   £ *13,600*

When interest is added to interest and capital it is known as 'compound' interest. The higher the rate of interest the faster the sum increases, e.g. £1,000 at 5% p.a. for 35 years produces £5,516 but £1,000 at 15% p.a. for 35 years produces £133,176 (i.e. over 24 times faster).

This illustrates how important it is for investors to select the 'right' type of investment particularly in times of high inflation. Economists use the phrase 'opportunity cost' (i.e. the opportunity cost of leaving cash in a wallet is the interest that could have been earned in a savings account). In order to advise fully, investment analysts must compare on an effective rate basis and must take account of (a) liquidity (ease with which one can liquidate in order to retrieve all capital), (b) the cost of buying into and selling out of alternatives, (c) the costs of managing alternative investments, and (d) the security of the capital and the income in real and money terms.

If you hold money in savings accounts your account will be made up every time you pay in or draw out or have interest added, as in Q1.6. When left to accumulate the interest is said to compound.

The theory of opportunity cost and compound interest is the foundation for the whole subject of investment analysis. It would be tedious and unnecessary to produce an annualised table every time one needed to know a future cost or value when it can be expressed algebraically; for example £100 invested earning interest at 6% will accumulate over 3 years as follows:

$$100 + (100 \times 0.06) = 106 \qquad \text{OR} \qquad 100(1.00 + 0.06) = 106$$
$$106 + (106 \times 0.06) = 112.36 \qquad\qquad 106(1.00 + 0.06) = 112.36$$
$$112.36 + (112.36 \times 0.06) = 119.10 \qquad 112.36(1.00 + 0.06) = 119.10$$

$$\text{OR} \quad 100(1.06)^3 = 119.10$$

This can be generalised into a compound interest formula, $(1 + i)^n$ where i = the rate of interest as a decimal per period of time and where n = the interest earning period of time.

Valuers refer to this compound interest formula as 'The Amount of £1' or the amount to which £1 invested at i will accumulate to after n periods of time. This can be expressed as $(1 + i)^n$ or A. Tables of this function and others have been produced e.g. Parry's valuation tables, Rose's valuation tables, Bowcock's valuation tables.

1.8 Using the formula $(1 + i)^n$ calculate the amount that:

    a) £100 invested for 4 years at 6% will accumulate to

                          £ _____

    b) £55,000 invested for 10 years at 10% will accumulate to

                          £ _____

    c) £3.35 invested for 15 years at 8% will accumulate to

                          £ _____

    d) £50 invested for 7 years at 5% nominal payable half yearly will accumulate to   £ _____

    e) £200 invested for 5 years at 5% effective payable monthly will accumulate to   £ _____

Many forms of saving involve investment of regular sums at regular intervals. 'Save as you earn' schemes are an example.

1.9 Mrs. Y has agreed to save £100 a year for 5 years at 11% p.a. She will deposit the first £100 in precisely 12 months' time. Complete the table overleaf to show how this scheme operates.

4

Amount at start of Year	Interest at end of year at 11%	Amount deposited at end of year	Amount with interest
1	0	0	100	100
2	100			
3				
4				
5				

NOTE: It is generally assumed that all financial events happen at the end of fixed regular periods of time, usually assumed to be annual. This need not be the case. Reconsider Q*1.9* as follows specifying the total sum accumulated at the end of 5 years in each case:

    a) £100 invested at the start of each year beginning to-day at an effective annual rate of 11%   £ _____

    b) £8.34 at the end of each month at 1% per month   £ _____

    c) £25 to-day plus a further £25 every 3 months at 3% every 3 months   £ _____

This regular saving and compounding can also be expressed algebraically and is called by valuers 'The amount of £1 per annum'.

$$A\ \pounds1\ \text{per annum} = \frac{(1 + i)^n - 1}{i}$$

1.10 Mr. X is 25 and has taken out a Life Assurance policy maturing when he is 60. He is required to pay an annual premium of £500 which will earn interest at 4.5%. Using formulae assess the amount payable on maturity

    a) assuming a first payment to-day
    b) assuming a first payment in 12 months' time.

The first two formulae can be used to calculate future sums of money given certain facts about present sums of money. The

5

reciprocal of the amount of £1 can be used to assess present values of future sums. The reciprocal of a number is 1 (unity) divided by that number.

e.g. the reciprocal number of 5 is one fifth or as a decimal 0.20.

The reciprocal of A = 1/A   i.e. $\dfrac{1}{(1 + i)^n}$

The reciprocal of A £ p.a. = $\dfrac{1}{\dfrac{(1 + i)^n - 1}{i}}$ or $\dfrac{i}{(1 + i)^n - 1}$

These functions of £1 are called respectively the Present Value of 1 (pound) or PV and the sinking fund factor or ASF (Annual Sinking Fund).

1.11 Mrs. Y has promised to pay Mr. X £5,000 in 5 years' time. Using the formulae or the appropriate valuation table calculate on a 7.5% basis:

    a) How much she needs to invest today.

                  £ _____

    b) How much she needs to invest at the end of each year.

                  £ _____

    c) Is b) cheaper than a)?   Yes/No

These two functions are frequently used by all investment analysts.

Remember provided there is only one missing piece of information then that missing piece can always be found.

1.12 Mrs. Y has been offered a short-term investment which will produce £860 annually in arrears for 5 years. What price (present value) should she pay for the investment to achieve a return of 7.5%?   £ _____

1.13 Demonstrate that in Q*1.12* Mrs. Y achieves a return on, and a return of, her capital at 7.5%. Use the following column headings.

(1) Year	(2) Capital outstanding (2 - 5)	(3) Interest @ 7.5%	(4) Income of £860	(5) Capital replaced (4 - 3)

Government Stocks, known in the Stock Exchange and financial press as Gilts or Gilt-edge securities, are considered by many to be the safest form of investment because (a) they are easily bought and sold, (b) they involve nominal purchase and management costs, (c) the income is guaranteed and safe (backed by Central Government), (d) the capital is safe if held to maturity.

Knowledge of present values (PV of £1) helps the analyst to measure and compare alternative investment opportunities such as stocks.

1.14 3% Treasury Stock maturing in 3 years can be purchased for £80 per £100 face value. Assess their rate of return by trial and error using the following lay-out.

Year	Benefits	PV of £1 at 10%	PV x Benefit
0	- £80	x1	- £80
1	+ £3 (3% on £100)	x	
2	+ £3	x	
3	+ £3	x	
	+ £100	x	
Sum of present values of benefits less costs		£	

If 10% produces a negative sum, try again at a lower rate %. If 10% produces a positive sum try again at a higher rate %. Do this two or three times until the present value sum is at or close to £0.

In practice this calculation can be carried out using a programmed financial calculator or a computer. This exercise represents a close encounter with Investment arithmetic as used by valuers. From it certain facts and definitions need to be noted.

NOTE:
    a) The term for this type of calculation is Discounted Cash Flow (DCF for short).
    b) A DCF exercise can be carried out using pre-selected rates of interest called the discount rates or the investor's required rate of return or the cost of capital.
    c) When a rate of return is found which produces a zero solution then that rate represents the investment's yield or rate of return. This is generally called the investment's Internal Rate of Return (IRR for short).
    d) The IRR of all stocks is called a Redemption Yield because it is the true return if held until redeemed (paid back at face value) by the Government on the due date. Undated stock are called irredeemable stock.

1.15 Calculate the price an investor should pay for 3% treasury stock maturing in 3 years if the investor requires a return of 15%.

Year	Benefit	PV of £1 at 15%	PV x Benefit
0			
1	+ £3		
2	+ £3		
3	+ £3		
	+ £100		
		Sum	£

When a pre-selected rate is used then the sum of the discounted amounts is called the Net Present Value (NPV) of that investment at that rate %. Here the NPV is the price an investor should pay if a 15% return is to be achieved. If it exceeds the market price of £80 (*1.14*) then buying at the market price will produce a return greater than 15% if held to redemption. If it is less than £80 buying at £80 will produce a return of less than 15%.

NOTE. All investors, because they are aware of the opportunity cost of saving money, will require both a return **ON** their money and the return **OF** their money.

1.16 An investor purchased a property 10 years ago for £62,500 and sold it yesterday for £500,000. For the first 5 years of ownership the rent received from the tenant was £5,000 at the end of each year and for the last 5 years it was £30,000 a year. What rate of return (IRR) did the investor enjoy? (Try 30% and 32%.)

1.17 A property owner must replace some lifts in 4 years time. Replacement lifts cost £20,000. If the owner can invest at 10% calculate (a) the lump sum investment to be made to-day, and (b) the annual sum of the alternative annual sinking fund.

    a) £ _____

    b) £ _____

    c) Is b) cheaper than a) Yes/No

1.18 If lift costs are rising by 12% per annum over the 4 years

    a) What will be the lump sum cost at 8% gross?
                        £ _____

    b) What will be the annual sinking fund at 8%
    gross?   £ _____

    c) Are tax and inflation important factors
    to be considered when making investment
    decisions?   Yes/No

    d) Why?

    e) What are the revised figures in a) and b) if
    tax on interest is at 25%?

There are many investments including property which produce constant cash flows over periods of time. To calculate such an investment's present value using only the PV of £1 would be laborious. But the PV of a constant cash flow can be found by first summating the PV Factors. For example, if an investment yields £100 at the end of each year for 6 years and a 10% return is required then the investment's present worth could be calculated as follows:

9

1 £100 x PV £1 in 1 year at 10% (.909)	=	£90.90
2 £100 x PV £1 in 2 years at 10% (.826)	=	£82.60
3 £100 x PV £1 in 3 years at 10% (.751)	=	£75.10
4 £100 x PV £1 in 4 years at 10% (.683)	=	£68.30
5 £100 x PV £1 in 5 years at 10% (.620)	=	£62.00
6 £100 x PV £1 in 6 years at 10% (.564)	=	£56.40
		£435.30

But .909 + .826 + .751 + .683 + .620 + .564 = 4.353 therefore the present value of £100 for 6 years at 10% = £100 x 4.353 = 435.30

This is generally set out to read:

Income	£100.00
x PV £1 p.a. for 6 years at 10%	4.353
PV of £100 for 6 years at 10%	£435.30

NOTE. 1. Tables of PVs for £1 per period have been calculated.
2. The Formula for such a table is $(1 - PV)/i$ where
$PV = 1/(1 + i)^n$ or $1/(i + ASF)$

One very important type of loan in the property world, and of particular concern to house buyers, is called a mortgage. A mortgage is a loan of money based on the security of the property to be purchased. Mortgages usually require the person borrowing to repay the loan over a fixed term, including interest at a specific (but usually variable) rate of interest. From the lender's viewpoint this is an exchange of capital for a specific cash flow. As such a mortgage is in effect an investment. For example, if Mr. and Mrs. X are borrowing £15,000 to help purchase a house and the loan is over 25 years at 12%, then the annual repayment of interest and capital can be found as follows:

Income to Building Society	£x p.a.

PV of £1 p.a. for 25 years at 12%	7.843
PV of £x p.a. for 25 years at 12%	7.843 x
But 7.843x = £15,000	
x = £ 1,912.53 per annum	

Again this is tedious but the annual sum can be found directly by using the reciprocal of the PV of £1 p.a. for 25 years, thus:

reciprocal of 7.843 = 1/7.843 = .1275

then	£ 15,000.00
x	.1275
Annual repayment of	£ 1,912.53

The reciprocal of the PV of £1 p.a. is the annuity £1 will purchase. In certain sets of tables this annuity factor is divided by 12 to produce the monthly constant which may be expressed in terms of £1 or £100.

1.19 a) Complete the following table (on a spare sheet of paper) to show how a standard loan or mortgage is repaid in this case over 25 years at 12%.

1(1-4)	2	3	4(3-2)
Loan outstanding at 12%	Interest on loan at 12%	Annual sum	Capital repaid
£15,000	1,800	1,912.53	112.50
£14,887.50	1,786.50	1,912.53	126.03
£14,761.47			

Any error in the final line will be due to rounding of figures to two decimal places.

b) What would happen to the payments if there was an increase in interest rates to 15% in year 5 (i.e. after 4 payments of £1,912.53)?

c) What would happen if, after 10 payments at 12% a further loan of £10,000 was obtained and the two loans had to be paid off in full at the end of the original term? Answer on the basis of
i) interest at 12%
ii) a rise in the rate to 15% after 5 payments.

1.20 a) What is the essential difference between a loan and a mortgage?

b) What is the essential difference between a repayment mortgage and an endowment mortgage?

c) How does tax relief help purchasers of residential property?

Summary

Investment Arithmetic is concerned with compound interest and the six functions of £1.

1. Amount of £1
2. Amount of £1 per period
3. Annual Sinking Fund
4. Present value of £1
5. Present value of £1 per period
6. a) Annuity £1 will purchase
   b) Mortgage or partial payment.

NOTE: These tables can, and are, used in conjunction with one another.

1.21 Work out the combination in the following cases:

a) What is the present value of an income of £1,000 p.a. for 5 years beginning in 5 years' time?

£ _____

b) If A invests £500 a year for 10 years at 8% and leaves the sum to accumulate for a further 10 years at 8%, how much will there be in 20 years?

£ _____

c) If A needs £5,000 in 5 years' time and can invest £1,000 now at 5%, what additional sum must be invested each year to achieve the aim?

£_____

There are two special points that have not been considered. The first is that the more frequently interest is added, given a nominal annual yield, the larger will be the accumulated sum. There is however a maximum sum possible. This is based on the concept of continuous compounding. Look this up in Baum and Mackmin.

The second is the fact that some incomes from some investments are perpetual, examples are irredeemable Government Stock and certain freehold interests in property where the income is fixed for an extensive period of years OR where, for simplicity, such an assumption can be made.

Substituting infinity for n in the PV £1 p.a. formula simplifies to give 1/i as the multiplier.

UK valuers have their own investment language. PV £1 p.a. is often called a figure of years' purchase or YP for short.

It should be noted that the formula for each function can be changed for (a) in advance assumptions (b) receipts or payments at other than annual intervals.

1.22   Your credit card charges interest at 2.5% per month. What is the effective rate per annum?

£ _____

In order to carry out an *Investment analysis* you require to know the investment income and the purchase price. Analysis by DCF produces the IRR (i.e. the yield or measure of that investment).

In order to carry out an *Investment valuation* you require to know the investment income and the appropriate rate of interest to discount the income and derive an estimate of market value.

In a *Property valuation or appraisal* you need to know the income, net of outgoings, and the market rate of interest used to discount the income to arrive at an estimate of market value.

All sectors of the investment market compete for funds and there is a well established relationship of yields in the market. These yields reflect the RISK of the various investments and tend to move in a specific direction, varying with money-market rates of interest and the effective level of demand in each sector of the market.

Questions dealing with the concept of dual rate and tax adjustments are considered in Section 4.

Test Paper

T.1. A sum of £250 is invested at 9½% for 15 years. What sum will there be at the end of 15 years? £ _____

T.2. A capital sum of £1,500 is needed in 10 years. How much must be invested today, assuming a compound rate of 8½%?
£ _____

T.3. A mortgage of £40,000 is arranged at 8%. What is the annual repayment if the term is for 30 years? £ _____

T.4. A sum of £1,000 is invested at the end of each year and earns interest at 16%. How much will this accumulate to in 10 years time? £ _____

T.5. How much must be invested each year at 6% compound interest to produce £2,500 in 16 years time? £ _____

T.6. You have expectations of becoming a partner in private practice in 10 years' time. This will cost you £25,000.

    a) How could you provide for this?
    b) How much would it cost at 12%? £ _____
    c) How much will it cost today saving at 12% if inflation is increasing the cost at 12%? £ _____

T.7. a) If you save £200 for 10 years at 7% depositing £200 each year in a Building Society - how much will you have at the end of 10 years? £ _____
    b) If you added a further lump sum of £2,000 at the beginning of Year 5 - how much will you have at the end of 10 years?
£ _____
    c) If you do (a) and (b) and leave it to accumulate for a further 5 years - how much will you have? £ _____

T.8. Friends have been offered the freehold interest in a good secondary shop let to newsagents. The newsagents are paying a rent of £10,000 a year for the next 5 years, after which it will rise to £50,000 in perpetuity. How much should your friends pay for the freehold if they want an 8% return? £ _____

T.9.   8% Treasury Stock are selling at £80 per £100 face value. What true rate of return does this represent? Assume redemption in 5 years.   £ _____

Chapter two

The income approach

When property is purchased it is an acquisition of a bundle of legal rights. The word property is used loosely to describe the specific rights in land that can be conveyed and or created in England and Wales. It is sometimes called REAL property.

Land (property) can be held Freehold, Leasehold or for life. A freehold, in legal terms the Fee Simple Absolute in possession, is an estate in land which is deemed to be perpetual and which can be freely conveyed to other persons. It may however be encumbered, e.g. by rights of way, and it may have to be conveyed subject to someone else's occupation rights because a leasehold interest has been created out of the freehold.

A leasehold estate in property has a finite duration, the length of the lease, and the leaseholder may be restricted by covenants in the lease in terms of use and freedom to assign or sub-let.

The key words in a property investment exercise are 'Income' and 'Yield'. Income refers to the freehold owner's actual, possible and or probable spendable income that is received, or could be received or may be received in the form of rent. The conversion of rent per annum to an estimate of capital value is known as capitalisation and is essentially a discounted cash flow exercise at a known rate of interest to arrive at that property's net present value.

The income to be discounted must in all cases be net spendable income. This phrase means that the appraiser must always check to see if the owner has to meet any expenditures in respect of the property out of rents received. These expenditures can relate to repairs, insurance, local taxes (rates) and owner's management expenses. Net in this case does *not* mean net of tax. Most property valuation is carried out on a before-tax basis.

Rent

The level of rent in an open market is determined by demand for that quality of space in that location for its permitted use. Estimates of rent can therefore be made by careful monitoring and analysis of known rents achieved on the letting of comparable premises.

16

Property must first be measured in accordance with the RICS code of measurement practice before the rent is analysed in terms of a rent per unit of comparison. In most cases the code suggests that rent should be analysed in terms of net lettable space. Roughly, this is the actual amount of space that can be used by an occupier for the purposes of his occupation. It excludes pillars, stairwells, circulation space and toilet facilities. These can reduce gross lettable space by 15 to 50%.

The unit of comparison used for offices, shops, factories and warehouses is the square foot or square metre.

2.1 If an office building of 10,000 sq. ft. net lettable space was let for £100,000 per annum, what rent per square foot was achieved?

£ _____

2.2 If a warehouse of 1,000 sq. metres was let for £50,000 what rent per square metre was achieved?   £ _____

Comparables must be analysed on a consistent basis. Before analysing a rent it is important to check net lettable space and the rent must be expressed in terms of net income, i.e. after allowing for owners' running costs, repairs, etc.

2.3 A first-floor office suite of 1,000 sq. ft. has just been let at £15,000 per annum. The landlord is liable for maintaining the structure and common parts, and insurance of the building. A service charge covers the cost of heating and lighting. Landlord's liability amounts to £3 per square foot. What is the effective net rental?   £ _____

Read up on the calculation of outgoings in Chapter 2.

Certain buildings have higher rents in some areas or floors than others. The two common examples being shops and multi-storey offices, factories and warehouses without adequate lifts. In a shopping street there will be considerable variations in size of units. The front section of all shops is considered to be the most valuable and on this presumption total net rent can be analysed to find the 'Zone A' rental which is then used as the unit of comparison.

2.4 Analyse on a zoning basis a net rent of £50,000 achieved on a recent letting of a shop measuring 6 metres by 30 metres.
Zone A rent =   £ _____

Old multi-storey factories, etc. can be handled in a similar way but here the zoning is vertical rather than horizontal. Understanding the letting market is one of the most difficult and most important tasks for a valuer.

Actual, possible and probable rent

Nearly every property can be classified, for valuation purposes, in one of the following groups and may in certain cases overlap two or more groups.

    A. Vacant buildings
        a) available for sale or letting
        b) held vacant awaiting development,
           redevelopment, or refurbishment
    B. Owner-occupied
    C. Occupied by tenants
        a) Paying current open market rents
        b) Paying rent which is below current open
           market rentals.

If a property is fully or partially let then examination of the leases will indicate 'how much rent is actually being collected by the freeholder'.

If a property is owner-occupied or vacant then the valuer must make an estimate of the possible rent if it were to be let.

If a property is let at less than market rent then the valuer can make an estimate of the probable level of rents when the current leases are renegotiated at rent review or on termination of the lease.

The assessment of rental value must precede the capital valuation of income producing property.

If a property is let, the lease(s) must be examined carefully to ascertain the landlord's liabilities in terms of repairs, insurance, management, etc.

At the conclusion of these preliminaries the valuer will have the basic information needed to prepare his or her valuation provided the valuer has sufficient experience of the market to know the current level of return on capital that is required by property investors. (See Chapter nine.)

Chapter three

The income approach to freeholds

Freehold valuation methodology has been the subject of much recent debate and is most fully discussed in Baum and Crosby, *Property Investment Appraisal*, Routledge 1988. In brief, conventional methods are growth implicit using a market capitalisation rate or all risks yield (ARY) to convert current estimates of rental value into an expression of capital value. Contemporary methods are growth explicit. In the latter methods the implied perpetual rental growth is derived from normal market data on capitalisation rates and equated yields. This information is used in the modified DCF approach to assess the implied reversionary rent and in the Crosby real value approach to assess an inflation risk free yield (IRFY) for deferment of the reversionary capital value. The two approaches produce similar results but are mutually exclusive.

Current market practice is to use a simple capitalisation approach on a term and reversion or layer basis using an equivalent or same yield throughout. The less comparable the subject property is to the market evidence the greater is the need for the valuer to exercise his or her skill in adjusting the equivalent yield. In these more unusual cases contemporary methods can produce interesting alternative opinions.

Figure 3.1 overleaf sets out a freehold valuation format for the conventional term and reversion approach, most valuers simplify this format. For simplicity most of the questions are based on net rents.

NOTE 1. The April 1989 VAT changes require the valuer to deduct any non-recoverable VAT and as always to capitalise net investment income.

2. If the property is fully let at market rental OR is owner occupied and could be fully let at market rental Part I income will be capitalised in perpetuity at a % and there will be no Part 2.

3. Part 2 may be repeated if the rent is to rise in stages. In such cases the intermediate steps will be capitalised using PV £1 p.a. for each term x by PV £1 for the appropriate terms. The final capitalisation will be in perpetuity deferred the total period of waiting.

Figure 3.1   Freehold property valuation format

Property Address
Client
Current (actual) rent passing £   Capitalisation rate   %
Open market rental   £
Rent review or lease renewal dates
Time from date of valuation to rent reviews or up until premises
are producing full rental value.

                                                 Value

1. Current rent   £
   less landlord's outgoings:

   a) Repairs   £
   b) Insurance   £
   c) Management   £
   d) Rates   £
   e) Other non-recoverable
      costs   _____

                Sub total_____ -£ _____

    Net of outgoings' income £

    x Present value of £1 p.a.
    for n years @   %   x _____   £ _____

2. Rent expected on review   £
   less landlord's outgoings:

   a) Repairs   £
   b) Insurance   £
   c) Management   £
   d) Rates   £
   e) Other non-recoverable
      costs   _____   -£ _____

    Net of outgoings' income   £ _____ C/F

Figure 3.1 (continued)

	£ B/F	Value
x PV of £1 p.a. in perpetuity @ %	x _____	
	£	
x PV of £1 for n years @ %	_____ + £ _____	
	£	
Plus present value of any lump sums (premiums) due to F/H	+ £ _____	
	£	
Less PV of any capital costs to be paid by the F/H (e.g. urgent repairs)	- £ _____	
Estimated capital value	£ _____	

NOTE 4. Part 2 can be re-written as:
    a) PV £1 p.a. in perpetuity deferred
      n years at % or
    b) PV £1 p.a. in perpetuity <u>less</u> PV
      £1 p.a. for period of waiting.

Using the preceding format set out your valuations of the following freehold properties using the information given.

3.1 Value the freehold interest in shop premises fully let at the current open market rental value of £20,000 p.a. The capitalisation rate is 5%. The tenant meets all other expenses.

3.2 Value the freehold interest in shop premises fully let at a rent of £10,000 p.a. with 5 years of the present lease to run. The open market rental value is £20,000 p.a. The tenant meets all other expenses. An equivalent or same yield of 5% is to be used.

3.3 Value the freehold interest in shop premises fully let at a rent of £12,000 p.a. with 5 years of the present lease to run. Under the present lease the freeholder has to pay for external repairs costing an average annual amount of £1,000, insurance at an annual premium of £500 and management costing 3% of rent collected. The open-market rental value is £20,000 p.a., tenant meeting all normal expenses. An equivalent or same yield of 5% is to be used.

3.4 Revalue *3.2* and *3.3* using the layer method.

In some cases market valuers will still seek to reflect the added security or the added risk that they perceive affects some part of the income flow by varying the rates per cent used in the valuation. This can be very misleading. There is very little theoretical justification for this in capitalisation exercises carried out at a correct equivalent yield. Nevertheless some valuers may still seek to 'top slice' an early minimal reversion.

Various abbreviations, terms and phrases are used by surveyors. Explain each of the following.

3.5 FRV, ERV

3.6 FRI

3.7 IRI

3.8 Inclusive

3.9 Exclusive

3.10 Net rent

3.11 Net-of-tax rent

3.12 Service charges (a) full
 (b) partial

Freehold capitalisation rates

Most valuation courses and examination questions require the student to analyse market sales to derive capitalisation rates. In questions *3.13* a), b), c), trial and error can be used to assess the rate(s) used in the original capitalisation exercise.

3.13 Find the freehold capitalisation rate or equivalent yield in the following cases:

a) The freehold interest in a modern factory let at its current open market rent of £ 15,000 p.a. on full repairing and insuring terms and sold for £ 225,000.

b) The freehold interest in a modern factory let at £ 10,000 p.a. on full repairing and insuring terms has just been sold for £ 200,000. The lease has two years to run and the current open market rental value is £ 15,000 p.a.

c) The freehold interest in a modern factory let at £ 12,000 p.a. on internal repairing and insuring terms has just been sold for £ 195,000. The lease has two years to run. The open market rental value on FRI terms is £ 15,000. What rate of return will the purchaser receive?

Sales information as shown in *3.13* provides the valuer with the information needed to assess appropriate capitalisation rates for different types of property.

The following table is a guide only to what is happening in some areas of the market at the time of writing, but as the market is always changing they could be incorrect by the time of printing.

Shops	Very good High Street	4% - 5%	Prime 4.5%
	High St. but off centre	5% - 6%	
	District centres	6% - 7%	
	Small parades, etc.	8%	
	Poor	10%	
Offices	City and West End	6% - 7%	Prime 5.50%
	London - other	7% - 8%	
	Out of London commercial centres, e.g. Reading	7%	
	Other main provincial	7% - 8%	
	Secondary	8% +	
Factories	Modern, near motorways, etc.	7%	Prime 6.50%
	Other single storey	8%	
	Multi-storey, etc.	10% +	
	Depressed areas	15% - 20%	

The capitalisation rate selected depends upon many factors, but, at a given point in time and given specific market conditions, the rate will vary according to property type, property location, property condition, tenant, terms of the lease, regularity of rent reviews, and potential for income and capital growth.

One of the areas of debate in the income approach relates to the use of market capitalisation rates (ARYs) to value properties with abnormally long reversion patterns. A property let at below FRV with an early reversion can be valued using an equivalent yield approximating to the ARY obtained from the sale of a comparable property let at FRV. However, in the absence of direct comparables it is very difficult to justify a valuation based on the subjective adjustment of an ARY when the underlet property has a reversion in 10 or more year's time.

In these circumstances it is suggested that a modified DCF or real value approach should be the preferred approach. (Chapter 3).

Two of the contemporary approaches rely upon the assessment of an implied rental growth rate (g) derived from the normal market capitalisation rate (k), the equated yield (e), sometimes referred to as the expected redemption yield or opportunity cost rate, and the normal rent review pattern (t).

3.14 Calculate the implied rental growth rate from

$$K = e - (ASF \times P) \quad \text{or} \quad (1+g)^t = \frac{YPperp@K - YPtyears@e}{YPperp@K \times PVtyears@e}$$

given that K is 6% (0.06); e = 12% (0.12), and t = 5 (years).

The modified DCF on a term and reversion requires the valuer to (a) capitalise the term income for the unexpired period at e%, (b) to calculate the rent on reversion using 'g' (ERV today x A £1 in n years at g%) and to capitalise that rent at K% deferred the term at e% and add a + b.

The real value approach requires the valuer to calculate the inflation risk free yield (IRFY) from $(1 + e/1 + g) - 1$ then to capitalise
(a) the current rent for the unexpired term at e%, (b) to capitalise the ERV in today's terms at K% deferred the term at the IRFY and add a + b.

3.15 Using the assumptions given in *3.14* value a freehold shop property let at £20,000 p.a., the ERV today on a 5 year rent review pattern is £40,000 p.a. the reversion is in 15 years' time. Use a modified DCF and real value approach.

3.16 a) What are the main arguments to put forward for using a modified DCF or real value approach for valuing freehold underlet interests in property?

b) What is the main reason given by valuers in defence of conventional capitalisation approaches?

Chapter four

The income approach to leaseholds

Owners of property do not always occupy property. Property investors buy property for the income and capital growth it may produce. Hence property is frequently occupied by tenants. The contract between owner (landlord) and occupier (tenant) is a lease.

At the turn of the century it was quite common for leases to be granted for 99 years or more at a fixed rent. At that time such an arrangement was considered 'good' from the owner's point of view because he had secured a good income and a certain investment. Indeed right up to the late 1950s long leases were still being granted.

In the last 30 years real growth and inflation have affected investors' judgement and a freehold interest in property where the rent has been fixed for a long term is now considered to be a poor investment because it fails to keep pace with inflation.

From a tenant's point of view inflation means that although they are liable to pay rent for occupation rights they may become owners of valuable leasehold rights.

For example if a High Street shop had been let 89 years ago for 99 years at £100 a year with no provision for variation in the lease terms then that lease is now marketable. Why? Because the same shop may now be worth, say, £50,000 a year. This means that the current tenant is occupying a trading pitch worth £50,000 a year for a payment of £100. In other words, that tenant is saving £49,900 a year. If the tenant wishes to move out of those premises they will find other traders willing to purchase the unexpired term of 10 years for a considerable sum of money. Alternatively, they may be able to borrow on the security of the lease, or they may be able to realise that capital by surrendering their remaining term to the landlord for a substantial consideration in exchange for a new lease at current market rent.

The valuation of such leasehold interests has always caused problems. At the current time several methods are in use. These methods are best understood by considering the historical development of leasehold valuation methods. In every method the first stage is to assess the 'Profit rent', i.e. the difference between the rent receivable and the rent payable.

Profit Rent

1. Assess current open market rental.
2. Check lease terms to see that the rent reserved in the lease is on the same lease terms as the open market rental. If not, adjust the open-market rental value to bring it into line with the lease rent.
3. 1 - 2 equals profit rent.

Example 1. Property is let at £1,000 per annum on full repairing and insuring terms. The open market rent on such terms is £2,000. The lease has 3 years to run.

Market rent	£2,000 FRI
Lease rent	£1,000 FRI
Profit rent	£1,000

Example 2. Property is let at £1,000 per annum on internal repairing and insuring terms. The open market rental is £2,000 per annum on the same terms. The lease has 3 years to run.

Market rent	£2,000 IRI
Lease rent	£1,000 IRI
Profit rent	£1,000

Example 3. Property is let at £1,000 per annum on internal repairing and insuring terms. The open market rental is £2,000 per annum on full repairing and insuring terms. The landlord's average annual cost of meeting his repairing obligation is £250 per annum.

Market rent	£2,000 FRI
Lease rent	£1,000 IRI
Profit rent unadjusted	£1,000
Repairing adjustment	250
Adjusted profit rent	£1,250

But preferred method:

Market rent	£2,250 IRI
Lease rent	£1,000 IRI
Profit rent	£1,250

This adjustment causes examinees as many problems as almost any other valuation issue. It is purely commonsense when looked at from a property owner or a tenant's point of view. The market is saying that a landlord is willing to accept £2,000 a year in rent provided the tenant meets all the other occupation costs. If the landlord is going to accept responsibility for some of those costs then a higher rent will have to be paid, i.e. £2,250.

Valuation Method

A leasehold interest in property is a wasting asset. At the end of the lease the tenant will have nothing. Before 1939 property was considered to be a more risky investment than government stocks. Leaseholds had an additional risk over freeholds - they had a terminal life and restrictive terms. In order to compensate for this risk the valuers used a higher remunerative rate than for an equivalent freehold and a lower % to provide for the return of capital than for the return on the leasehold investment. This resulted in the production of leasehold valuation tables.

By the 1940s valuers had begun to look at tax implications on leaseholds. It seemed obvious that if the profit rent had to provide both a return on the investment and a return of the acquisition cost then the latter must reflect that the return of capital would have to be met out of taxed income. Hence leasehold tables adjusted for tax.

Today it is argued that as most purchasers of leasehold investments are tax exempt it is unnecessary to make the tax adjustment.

Read Baum and Mackmin, Chapter 4 and answer the following questions.

4.1 Value a leasehold interest in shop premises let at £5,000 per annum on internal repairing and insuring terms. The lease has 7 years to run. The full rental value is £8,000 on full repairing and insuring terms. Assume a leasehold rate of 7% and a sinking fund of 3% adjusted for tax at 40p. Demonstrate that after allowing for tax on the gross sinking fund payment and for tax on the sinking fund interest the investor achieves a 7% gross return on the estimated purchase price.

An arithmetic problem arises where there is a variable profit rent and a dual rent capitalisation is to be used. Several methods for overcoming this are set out in the main text. Of these the sinking fund method is the most accurate. A popular alternative is Pannell's method. Here the capital value of the variable profit rents are found by capitalising each on a single rate basis using the appropriate leasehold remunerative rate(s). The annual equivalent of the product is then found by dividing though by the YP for the full unexpired term at the remunerative rate or the average of the rates used. This annual equivalent can then be capitalised on a dual rate basis for the full term.

4.2 a) Value a leasehold interest at 8% and 4% adjusted for tax at 40%, the profit rent is £1,000 for 5 years and rises to £1,250 for a further 5 years.
b) Revalue using the sinking fund method or Pannell's method.

4.3 Distinguish between the valuation of a leasehold interest on assignment (e.g. Retailer A selling his lease of a High Street location to Retailer B) and the valuation of a leasehold investment producing a fixed profit rent for 5 years.

4.4 The dual rate approach to leasehold valuation should be abandoned because ....
and a single rate net of tax approach adopted because ....
....

   Conventional dual rate methods cannot sensibly deal with the problem of geared profit rents.

4.5 What valuation problem has to be solved when valuing a head leasehold interest with 20 years to run with one review to open market rent in 5 years. The property is sub-let for the full term less one day with rent reviews every 5 years beginning in 5 years' time? What is the contemporary solution to such a problem?

Chapter five

Taxation and valuation

In the market place freehold interests are normally valued on a before tax basis, leasehold interests on a dual rate adjusted for tax basis (Chapter 4). In terms of investment analysis 'before' and 'after' tax returns may have to be calculated at the client's tax rate.

5.1 A pension fund paying tax at 0% has just purchased a leasehold investment producing a fixed profit rent of £100,000 p.a. for £200,000. The lease has 4 years to run. What rate of return (IRR) will the fund receive from the investment?

5.2 An investor has just paid £1m. for a piece of land on the edge of a small town. Ignoring the income from pony grazing, assess the net of tax return after the land is sold in 3 years' time for development for £10m. Capital gains tax at 40p in the pound is payable.

VAT

The VAT changes announced in the Finance Bill 1989 require valuers to be even more careful in their assessment of net investment income.

A number of new issues are emerging, a few of which can be noted, but all await amplification in the market.

1. In some cases, but not in all, previous non-recoverable VAT on landlords' repairs and agents' fees may become recoverable increasing net income.

2. A surrender of a lease may become a chargeable supply; where it does it will need to be reflected in negotiations, and if the VAT thereon is not recoverable it may affect surrender values.

3. The effect on development appraisal is problematic depending upon the assumed VAT status of the developer and tenant and proposals for letting and/or disposal.

4. VAT will be payable on some sales and vatable owners may elect to charge VAT on rent.

Chapter six

Landlord and tenant valuations

Premiums

A premium is a capital sum paid in exchange for more favourable lease terms. It is the present worth of rent foregone (FH) or profit rent obtained (LH).

There are shorthand methods of calculating a premium but the preferred approach is based on the premise that:

value of present interest = value of proposed interest

6.1 During negotiations for the lease of a factory the tenant indicates willingness to pay a premium in lieu of rent. The lease is for 5 years. The open market rental is £5,000. The proposed premium is £2,000.

a) Calculate the reduced rental that should be reserved in the lease.

b) If the freeholder would only accept a reduced rent of £2,500 what premium would the tenant have to pay?

Future costs and receipts

If it is clear from the full analysis of the property interest being valued that ownership will require substantial expenditure or will result in substantial future receipts of capital then these must be reflected in the valuation. Some cases can be listed:

1. Agreed premiums. These add to the value of recipients' interest and reduce the value of the payer's interest. Immediate payments have to be allowed for by addition to or subtraction from value. If premiums are agreed future sums, then their net present value (FV x PV = NPV) must be added to the recipient's value and deducted from payer's value. The discount rate should be the current money rate.

2. Immediate capital expenditure on repairs, etc. should be deducted from the capital value.

3. Future capital expenditures on repairs, etc. must also be allowed for; these have an uncertain element. It is usually possible to assess the cost today, e.g. How much will it cost today to replace the central heating boiler? But the problem is more likely to be - How

much will it cost to replace the boiler at the end of its life in 5 years' time?

If the cost today is £5,000 what will be the cost in 5 years' time? The answer is generally more than £5,000. To project forward and then to discount back will produce near enough a figure of £5,000. So it is probably sensible to deduct the £5,000 now, making a small adjustment for the boiler's remaining life.

The traditional method of discounting the 'today cost' for the period of time at the capitalisation rate should not be used.

Marriage value

Marriage or merger value is said to exist when the bringing together of different ownerships in property produces a higher value than the sum of those different legal rights. The simplest example is the acquisition of existing buildings for redevelopment purposes. But marriage value can exist if the market value of the freehold interest let at open market rental is greater than the sum of existing freehold and leasehold interests valued separately.

6.2 To what extent is marriage value a phenomenon of valuation methods? To what extent is it the result of market imperfections?

Extensions and renewals of leases

6.3 The tenant of a workshop has a lease with 3 years' unexpired at a net rent of £5,000 a year. The FRV on FRI terms is £20,000 a year. Using a freehold rate of 10% and a leasehold rate of 12% and 3% adjusted for tax at 40p assess the new rent to be paid on surrender of the lease for a new 10 year lease with a rent review after 5 years.

Non-standard rent reviews

6.4 A landlord is willing to let property on a 10 year term without rent review provided the agreed rent for the full term is equivalent to that which would have been paid with a review after 5 years. Solve, on the basis of a normal rent of £10,000 p.a., an equated yield of 12% and an expected growth rate of 10% p.a.

Chapter seven

Legislation and the income approach

At this point the reader must apply his or her understanding of the principles of the income approach to the real world where the relationship of landlord and tenant may be affected by statute.

Leasehold enfranchisement

7.1 Your client is the owner-occupier of a long leasehold interest in a house. Their occupation fulfills all the requirements for enfranchisement. The ground rent is £20 p.a., the lease has 5 years to run, the open market freehold value is £150,000, an open market rent would be £15,000 p.a. net, a fair rent after deduction of expenses would have produced £5,000 p.a. net. Assess the enfranchisement price assuming they qualify (a) under the 1967 Act; (b) under the 1974 Act.

Landlord and Tenant Acts 1927 and 1954

7.2 Your client owns the freehold interest in an office building. The building has a ground floor and four upper floors and the whole is held on full repairing and insuring terms for 21 years without reviews. The lease has 3 years to run at £150,000 p.a.

The building originally contained only a ground and two upper floors but the tenant agreed as a condition of the lease to add a third floor. This work was completed within 2 years of the grant at a cost of £150,000. Seven years ago a mansard roof was added at a further cost of £50,000. All these works were approved by the landlord.

There are 400m^2 on each of the ground, first, second and third floors but the top floor, which is of mansard construction, has an area of only 250m^2.

Office space is letting at £200 per m^2. Where there is no lift, the rent on upper floors is £150 per m^2.

The property is assessed for rating at a 1990 RV £350,000. Freehold equivalent yields are 7%.

The tenants now wish to refit and equip the building with new carpets, lighting, computer, etc., but before proceeding wish to improve their security of tenure. They would prefer to buy the freehold but as a second best would like to surrender their present lease for a new 20 year full repairing and insuring lease with reviews every 5 years.

Advise the freeholder, ignoring VAT:
a) on the rent he could expect to get in 3 years' time;
b) on the price he should ask for the freehold interest;
c) on the rent he should ask for the proposed 20 year lease;
d) on the amount of compensation he would have to pay the tenant if he were able to recover possession.

Chapter eight

Development appraisal

Many developers now have their own computer software for development appraisal studies. In all such studies the greatest problem is determining the best scheme of development and the principal costs and benefits. The question that follows is grossly simplified to provide the reader with an appreciation of the fundamental points only.

8.1 Assess the residual site value of a parcel of land suitable for 5,000m^2 (gross) of office space. The scheme will take 12 months to complete. Rents are £200 per m^2 net lettable area. Construction costs are £400 per m^2. The scheme would sell on a 7% basis and finance is available at 14%. Promotion costs are budgeted at £40,000. Letting fees at 15% of the first year's rent. Purchase costs are 1.75%, site purchase costs 1.5%, stamp duty 1%. Agents' sale fees are 1% of GDV. Developers' profit is 15% of GDV.

Chapter nine

Analysis

When appraisers are instructed to give advice on investment opportunities, the investor is seeking advice on expected yields. In such cases the valuer must take account of acquisition costs. The main costs are legal fees, stamp duty on conveyancing, appraisal fee including surveys; in total these can range from 2.75% to 4%.

In the case of Government Stock an actual future redemption yield can be calculated on the assumption that the stock is held until redemption. In the case of property a future redemption yield can only be assessed after the valuer has made a number of assumptions, namely:

1. Future levels of rent for at least 15 years, based on economic analysis of the property type within its locality. Normally a growth rate is assumed and future rental value is calculated using the A £1 table or the assessment is based on implied rental growth.

2. Future redemption value (i.e. the amount the investor hopes to receive if the property is sold at the end of the projected period). The rental value used is the final figure obtained in 1. The capitalisation rate used will frequently be the same as that at the date of analysis but it may be moderated in line with current economic projections. This value may be called the terminal value.

9.1 A property has just been sold for £1 million freehold. It is currently producing a rent of £60,000 p.a. net. The full rental value is £110,000 p.a. The lease will be renewed in 4 years' time. Assuming all further information, calculate the following:

a) total acquisition costs;

b) current return based on purchase price plus acquisition costs;

c) expected return after the lease is renewed;

d) the capitalisation rate(s) used by the valuer;

e) the internal rate of return assuming rental growth at 5% per annum and a re-sale in 4 years' time; assuming no change in capitalisation rate;

f) the growth in rental value needed over the next 4 years

   i) in pounds

  ii) as a rate of growth per annum in order to achieve a redemption yield (IRR) equivalent to short dated stock of 12%.

9.2 Define:
a) IRR;
b) gross redemption yield;
c) equivalent yield;
d) equated yield.

In the author's opinion, readers arriving at this point without error, omission or misunderstanding now require a minimum of 5 years' market experience working with a Chartered Valuation Surveyor before being in a position to undertake independently an investment valuation of property competently. To do so and offer appraisal opinions they will need to have been elected an Associate member of the Royal Institution of Chartered Surveyors or the Incorporated Society of Valuers and Auctioneers.

Solutions

Some solutions are absolute but, as in real life, perfectly valid alternative opinions might be possible in some cases. The important point is to appreciate the reasoning behind the solutions given.

1.1 £40.00   *1.2* £225.00: £225.00

1.3

600	5	1	(30)
1,000	(9)	1	90
(2,000)	20	1	400
57.50	14	1	(8.05)

1.4 NO a) £450 b) £460.13 c) £469.03

1.5 a) 12.68% b) 12.55% c) 12.36%

1.6 $100 + 10 = 110 + 11 = 121 + 12.10 = 133.10 + 13.31 = 146.41 + 14.64 = 161.05$

1.7 $10,000 + 1,200 = 11,200 + 1,344 = 12,544 + 1,505 = 14,049$

1.8 £126.25 : £142,665.84 : £10,626 : £70,648 : £255.26
(as the rate is effective there is no need to find the rate % per month).

1.9

1	0	0	100	100
2	100	11	100	211
3	211	23.21	100	334.21
4	334.21	36.76	100	470.07
5	470.97	51.81	100	622.78

a) £691.29 b) £681.13 c) £691.89

1.10 a) £42,581.98   b) £40,748.34

1.11 a) £3,482.19 (PV) b) £860.82 (ASF)
c) NO, because both have the same present value at 7.5%

1.12 £3,479.47
$(860 \times PV^1 + 860 \times PV^2 + 860 \times PV^3 + 860 \times PV^4 + 860 \times PV^5$
OR $860 \times PV$ £1 pa. at 7.5% for 5 years)

1.13

Year	Capital	Interest at 7.5%	Income	Capital replaced
1	£3,479.47	260.96	860	599.04
2	£2,880.43	216.03	860	643.97
3	£2,236.46	167.73	860	692.27
4	£1,544.19	115.81	860	744.19
5	£ 800.00	60.00	860	800.00

1.14 Sum at 10% is £ 11.95. Internal Rate of Return is 11.21%

1.15 Price is £ 72.60.

1.16 Set out as a PV exercise such as *1.15* the IRR is 31.43%. With a calculator try using high speed NPV e.g. 530,000 ÷ 1.30 + 30,000 ÷ 1.30 ....
.... + 5,000 ÷ 1.30 - 62,500 = NPV of 5,626. Therefore try 32% (1.32) and interpolate.

1.17 a) £ 13,660.27 b) £ 4,309.40 c) No, because they both have the same PV and FV.

1.18 First calculate FV at 12% inflation using $(1+i)^n$
    a) £ 26,491.15 b) £ 7,366.97 c) Yes d) Ignoring inflation and tax could produce misleading results for a client which could result in incorrect decisions.
    e) £ 24,927.07, £ 7,193.73.

1.19 a) Recheck if last line capital repaid does not equal last line loan outstanding.
    b) Capital at beginning of year 5 is £ 14,462.55 (1,912.53 x PV £ 1 p.a. for 21 years at 12%) therefore at 15% repayments must rise to £ 2,291.16 p.a. (14,462.55 x A £ 1 w.p. for 21 years at 15% x 0.15842 = £ 2,291.16).
    c) i) Capital to be repaid after 10 years at 12% is £ 10,806.177 plus £ 10,000 gives £ 20,806.177 for 15 years at 12% which is £ 3,054.84 p.a.
        ii) After 5 years (i.e. beginning of year 6) capital owed is £ 14,285.15. After 5 more years repaying at 15% capital is £ 13,345.38 plus £ 10,000 gives £ 23,345.38 for 15 years at 15% which is £ 3,992.44 p.a.

1.20 a) A mortgage is a loan secured on property.
    b) A repayment mortgage repays interest and capital each year of the mortgage. An endowment provides for repayment of capital at the end of the loan period through an endowment assurance policy.
    c) It reduces the interest payments to a net tax level, under the MIRAS arrangements the repayments are calculated on a net of tax rate of interest.

1.21 a) £ 3,146.36 b) £ 15,637.69 c) £ 673.60

1.22 34.48% $([1.025]^{12} - 1) \times 100$.

TEST PAPER

T.1 £ 975.33 (A £ 1) *T.2* £ 663.429 (PV £ 1)

T.3 £ 3,553.20 (Annuity x. or PV £ 1 p.a. ÷) *T.4* £ 21,321.44 (A £ 1 p.a.)

T.5 £ 97.38 (ASF)

T.6 a) Lump sum or annual sinking fund b) £ 8,049.25 or £ 1,424.60 p.a.
c) £ 25,000 x A £ 1 at 12% = £ 25,000 x 3.1058 = £ 77,645 x PV £ 1 at 12% = £ 25,000). Therefore £ 25,000 or £ 4,424.59.

T.7 a) £ 2,763 (A £ 1 p.a.) b) £ 5,764.75 c) £ 8,085.36

Solutions

T.8 £465292 (10,000 x PV £1 p.a. @ 8% + 50,000 x PV £1 p.a. in perp. @ 8% x PV £1 in 10 years @ 8%)

T.9 13%

2.1 £10 per sq. ft.   *2.2* £50 per sq. metre   *2.3* £12,000 or £12 sq. ft.

2.4 £574.71 say £575 using Zone A+B depths of 7M and Zone C remainder, halving back.

3.1 £400,000 (20,000 x YP perp. @5%)

3.2 £356,705 (10,000 x YP for 5 yrs. @5% + 20,000 x YP perp. def'd 5 yrs. @5%)

3.3 £357,000 (i.e. term income net of outgoings comparable to *3.2*)

3.4 Same solution on an equivalent yield basis.

3.5 Full rental value (RR = Rack rental) (ERV = Estimated rental value)

3.6 Full repairing and insuring   *3.7* Internal repairing and insuring

3.8 Inclusive of rates   *3.9* Exclusive of rates

3.10 Net rent = net of landlord's outgoings

3.11 Net of outgoings and income or corporation tax

3.12 a) All landlord's costs on heatings and lighting etc. recovered from tenants.
b) Only those stated in the lease are recoverable.

3.13 a) 6.67%   b) 7.2% (try 7% and 7.25%)   c) 7.35% (try 7% and 7.5%)

3.14 $(1+g)^5 = \dfrac{16.6667 - 3.6048}{16.6667 \times 0.56743} = \dfrac{13.0619}{9.4571} = \sqrt[5]{\ } 1.38115 = 1.38115^{0.2} =$
$1.066716 - 1 \times 100 = 6.67\% = g$

3.15

D.C.F.		20,000		Real Value	20,000		
YP 15 yrs @ 12%		6.8109	136,218		6.8109	136.218	
Reversion to Implied		105,364			40.000		
(40,000 x A £1 in 15 yrs. @ 6.67)							
YP perp @ 6%				YP perp @ 6%			
PV £1 in 15 yrs				PV £1 in			
@ 12%		3.045	320.839	15 yrs @ 5%*	8.017	320.686	
ECV			£457,057			£456,904	

* this is the IRFY calculated from $1 + e / 1 + g - 1 = 0.049967 \times 100 = 4.9967\%$ say 5%

the variation in the two approaches is due to rounding in the calculations.

3.16 a) i) the longer the reversion the more difficult it is to find a true comparison.

40

ii) the longer the reversion the more difficult it is to justify the valuer's subjective adjustment of the ARY and/or the use of non-standard approaches.

iii) conventional capitalisation includes the capitalisation of the term at a growth capitalisation rate when clearly there can be no growth in a contracted rent.

iv) on the basis of investor indifference. provided the same equated yield is achieved, then a contemporary approach produces the investor's indifferent purchase price.

b) i) the market values on a conventional basis.

ii) investors are not indifferent - market sales suggest that investors require a higher equated yield from long reversions. Thus subjective adjustment to equivalent yields may be as correct an approach as subjective adjustment to equated yields.

4.1

Full rental value	£ 8,000	FRI
Rent reserved	5,000	IRI
	3,000	
Adjust for variations in outgoings	1,000	
Profit rent	4,000	
YP 7 years at 7%/3% tax 40p	3.4781	
	£ 13,912	

CV £ 13,912
Gross Income £ 4,000
Net Income £ 2,400

Net spendable income
0.042 x 13,912
= £ 584.30

x Amt £ 1 p.a.
for 7 yrs. at 3%

Sinking fund
£ 2,400-584.30
=   £ 1,815.70

7.6625
£ 13.912

(Note: £ 4,000 - gross ASF of £ 3026 = £ 974 gross spendable income and [974 ÷ 13,912] x 100 = 7%)

4.2   a) Term profit rent

Term profit rent	1.000	
YP 5 years @ 8%/3% tax 40p	2.5386	£ 2,538
Reversion profit rent	1,250	
YP 5 years @ 8%/3% tax 40p		
PV £ 1 in 5 years @ 8%	1.727	£ 2,159
		£ 4,697

Here the money available for sinking fund investment will accumulate to more than £ 4,697 and the valuer advising the vendor will have undersold the investment.

Solutions

b) i) Sinking fund method

Let capital value = £x

Next 5 years' profit rent = £1.000

Gross SF $\quad$ = total income - spendable income (8%)

$\quad\quad\quad\quad$ = 1.000 - 0.08x

Net SF $\quad\quad$ = (1.000 - 0.08x) 0.6 (40p tax)

$\quad\quad\quad\quad$ = 600 - 0.048x

Remaining 5 years profit rent = £1.250

Gross SF $\quad\quad$ = 1.250 - 0.08x

Net SF = (1.250 - 0.08x) 0.6

$\quad\quad\quad\quad$ = 750 - 0.048x

The net SF accumulation is:

Next 5 years			600-0.048x
x A £1 p.a. 5 years @ 3%	5.3091		
x A £1 in 5 years @ 3%	1.1593	6.154	3.693-0.2954x
Remaining 5 years		750-0.048x	
x A £1 p.a. 5 years @ 3%		5.3091	3.982-0.2548x
			7.675-0.5502x

$$\text{Therefore } x = 7.675 - 0.5502x$$
$$1.5502 = 7675$$
$$x = £4.951$$

b) ii) Pannell's short cut

Next 5 years		1.000	
YP 5 years @ 8%		3.9927	£3.993
Remaining 5 years		1.250	
YP 5 years @ 8%	3.9927		
PV £1 in 5 years @ 8%	0.68058	2.717	£3.397
ECV single rate			£7.390

Therefore £7.390 ÷ YP 10 years @ 8% =	£1.101
YP 10 years @ 8%/3% tax 40p	4.4369
	£4.885

As a short cut it is effective but not accurate; compare £4.885 with £4.951.

4.3 Fixed profit rent for 5 years must be treated as short-term financial investment with much higher risk than 5 year dated Government Stock - so value at say 5% above short-dated yields. May be attractive to tax exempt funds.

Assignment of retail lease may include key money, goodwill and extra premium or overbid by special purchaser. Also profit rent to an owner-occupier under a lease is a variable rent which in good times rises year by year.

4.4 It was developed to answer a specific problem in the depression of the 1920s which may not be relevant to the recession of the 1980s. Net of tax single rate is the most obvious alternative technique.

4.5 Conventional dual rate only values the profit rent for the first 5 years because after that the head rent and sub lessees rent are the same and there is no profit rent. However, at the 10th and 15th years with real growth and/or inflation the profit rent could re-emerge. But the freeholder at year 5 might require an 'uplift' in rent to compensate for the fixed period of 15 years. This could produce a negative profit rent. Every leasehold is an individual investment opportunity and may have to be considered on a real value basis or full explicit DCF.

5.1 $\underline{\text{Capital Value}}$ = year's purchase
Income
$\dfrac{200,000}{100,000}$ = 2 year's purchase

Therefore YP 4 years @ x% = 2
x% = 34.90%

5.2 No precise calculation is possible because of the indexation adjustment that has to be made. This cannot be ascertained until the sale date. Therefore, assuming indexation at 7% per annum over the next 3 years and assuming purchase costs of 3% and sale costs of 2% the calculation could be :

Sale Price	£ 10,000,000	
Less sale costs 2%	200,000	£ 9,800,000
Less indexed purchase	£ 1,000,000	
Plus purchase costs 3%	30,000	
	£ 1,030,000	
x A £ 13 years at 7% (indexation)	1.225	£ 1,261,794
Realised gain		£ 8,538,205
Less tax at higher rate of 40%		£ 3,415,282
Net gain		£ 5,129,923

Solutions

6.1 a)

Full rental value	£ 5,000		
Premium	£ 2,000		

Freeholder's viewpoint

Present interest	£ 5,000		
YP perp at 7%	14.2857		£ 71,428.50
Proposed interest	£ x		
YP for 5 yrs @ 7%	4.1002	4.1002x	
Reversion to	£ 5,000		
YP perp def'd 5 yrs @ 7%	10.8985	54,492.5	
		£ 54,492.5 + 4.1002x	
Plus premium	£ 2,000		
		£ 56,492.5 + 4.1002x	

$$\text{Present} = \text{Proposed}$$
$$£ 71,428.5 = £ 56,492.5 + 4.1002x$$
$$x = £ 3,642.75$$

Tenant's viewpoint

Present interest		0
Proposed interest		
FRV	£ 5,000	
Rent to be reserved	x	
Profit rent	£ 5,000-x	
YP 5 years @ 8%/		
3% Tax 40p	2.5386	
	£ 12,693 - 2.5386x	
Less premium	£ 2,000	
	£ 10,693 - 2.5386x	

$$\text{Present} = \text{Proposed}$$
$$0 = £ 10,693 - 2.5386x$$
$$x = £ 4,212.16$$

Therefore rent will be agreed between £ 3,642.75 and £ 4,212.16

b)

Freeholder's viewpoint

Present interest as before			£ 71,428.50
Proposed interest	£ 2,500		
YP for 5 years @ 7%	4.1002	10,250.50	
Reversion	£ 5,000		
YP perp def'd			
5 years @ 7%	10.8985	54,492.5	
		£ 64,743	
+ Premium		x	
		£ 64,743 + x	

$$\text{Present} = \text{Proposed}$$
$$£ 71,428.5 = £ 64,743 + x$$
$$£ 6,685.5 = x$$

Tenant's viewpoint

Present interest		0
Proposed interest		
Full rental value	£ 5,000	
Rent to be reserved	£ 2,500	
Profit rent	£ 2,500	
YP 5 years @ 8%/		
3% Tax 40p	2.5386	
	£ 6,346.50	
Less premium	x	
	£ 6,346.5 - x	

Present = Proposed
0   = £ 6,346.5 - x
x   = £ 6,346.5

Here it would seem that there is no room for negotiation but in practice a figure of £ 6,500 might be agreed even though it is a notional loss to both parties.

6.2 The use of net-of-tax dual rate for leaseholds combined with before-tax single rate for freeholds largely accounts for the arithmetic presence of marriage value.

Very short leaseholds may well be unsaleable but traditional methods place a value on the interest. Similarly there is a reluctance in the market place to give full value to substantial early reversionary properties because of the low initial yields.

Marriage value undoubtedly exists in appropriate cases where adjoining sites are merged. It also exists in those cases where very clearly the market places different risk factors on the freehold and leasehold interests in a property. The latter is the most questionable owing to the lack of true market comparables and the difficulty of making acceptable subjective adjustments.

6.3 Freehold present interest

Next 3 years	£ 5,000	
YP 3 years @ 10%	2.4869	£ 12,434
Reversion	£ 20,000	
YP perp def'd 3 years @ 10%	7.5131	£ 150,262
		£ 162,696

Freehold proposed interest	£ x	
YP 5 years @ 10%	3.7908	£ 3.7908x
Reversion	£ 20,000	
YP perp def'd 5 years @ 10%	6.2092	£ 124,184
		£ 124,184 + 3.7908x

Therefore present = proposed
£ 162,696   = £ 124,184 + 3.7908x
£ 38,512   = 3.7908x
£ 10,159   = x

Solutions

Tenant's present interest

Next 3 years	£ 20,000
Less rent reserved	5,000
Profit rent	£ 15,000
YP 3 years 12%/3% tax 40p	1.5170
	£ 22,755

Tenant's proposed interest	£ 20,000 - £ x
YP 5 years 12%/3% tax 40p	2.3045
	£ 46,090 - 2.3045x

Therefore
$$£ 22,755 = £ 46,090 - 2.3045x$$
$$2.3045x = £ 23.335$$
$$x = £ 10,125$$

Agreement should be reached at about £ 10,000.

6.4

$$K = \frac{(1+r)^n - (1+g)^n}{(1+r)^n - 1} \times \frac{(1+r)^t - 1}{(1+r)^t - (1+g)^t}$$

$$K = \frac{(1+0.12)^{10} - (1+0.10)^{10}}{(1+0.12)^{10} - 1} \times \frac{(1+0.12)^5 - 1}{(1+0.12)^5 - (1+0.10)^5}$$

$$K = \frac{(3.11) - (2.59)}{3.11 - 1} \times \frac{(1.76) - 1}{(1.76) - (1.61)}$$

$$K = \frac{0.52}{2.11} \times \frac{0.76}{0.15}$$

$$K = 0.25 \times 5.07$$

$$K = 1.27$$

Therefore rent is £ 10,000 × 1.27 = £ 12,700.

7.1 a) Enfranchisement price under Leasehold Reform Act 1967

Existing ground rent	£ 20	
YP 5 years @ 6%	4.2124	£ 84

Reversion to modern ground rent		
Open market value	£ 150,000	
Site value @ 40%	£ 60,000	
Ground rent @ 6%	£ 3,600	
YP perp def'd 5 years @ 6%	12.4543	£ 44,835
Enfranchisement price, say		£ 44,919

Capitalisation rates from Lands tribunal and leasehold valuation tribunal decisions tend to be at 6-7%, the modern ground rent can be found, as here, by decapitalising a proportion of the open market vacant-possession value or by decapitalising a figure of site value from comparison or, rarely, by going direct to a modern ground rent by comparison. Decapitalising and capitalising at differential rates is no longer accepted by the courts. If the property has development value the

46

reversion is to development value deferred the unexpired term less the cost of compensating the leaseholder which can be taken to be the 50 year profit rent (ERV - modern ground rent) deferred the unexpired term.

b)   Enfranchisement price under Housing Act 1974 - standard approach

Existing ground rent		£ 20	
YP 5 years @ 6%		4.212x	£ 84

Reversion to net rent	Fair rent	
	5,000	
YP perp def'd 5 years @ 12%	4.7286	
	£ 23,643	

Plus half share of marriage gain		
Open market value		£ 150,000
Present freehold interest		£ 23,727
Leasehold interest	£ 15,000	
Less ground rent	20	
	£ 14,980	
YP 5 years @ 14%/3%		
tax 40%	2.2030	
	£ 33,000	

Marriage value is   £ 150,000-(23,727 + 33,000) = £ 93,273 ÷ 2 = £ 46,636

Therefore enfranchisement price is   £ 84 + £ 23,643 + £ 46,636 = £ 70,363

This is based on the Duke of Norfolk case. part of the argument being that in the absence of the Leasehold Reform Act 1967 the tenant would have held over under the Landlord and Tenant Act 1954 Part I which would have been at a 'fair' rent. However the changes caused by the Housing Act 1988 as amended by the Local Government and Housing Act 1989 S.186 and Schedule 10 and 11 where. after 15th January 1990 long leases under the Landlord and Tenant Act 1954 will continue as Assured periodic tenancies suggests that the calculations of the enfranchisement price for those leases due to terminate after 15th January 1990 will need to take account of this fact.

7.2   a) Full rental value of the building as improved:

4th floor	$250m^2$ x 200 =	50.000
Ground. 1st. 2nd. 3rd floors	4 x $400m^2$ x 200 =	320.000
		£ 370.000

S.34 market rent disregarding improvements:

1st. 2nd.3rd floors	3 x $400m^2$ x 150 =	180.000
Ground	$400m^2$ x 200 =	80.000
		£ 260,000

Probable rent in 3 years on current values: £ 260,000

b) The freehold interest:

Law of Property Act 1969 - 21 year rule

7 years	3	14 years	Perpetuity
IMPS	now £ 150,000	£ 260,000	£ 370,000

Landlord's present interest:			
Current net income		£ 150,000	
YP 3 years @ 7%		2.6243	£ 393,645
Reversion to S.34 rent*		£ 260,000	
YP 14 years @ 7%	8.7455		
PV £ 1 in 3 years @ 7%	.81630	7.1389	£ 1,856,127
Reversion to ERV		£ 370,000	
YP perp def'd 17 years @ 7%		4.5225	£ 1,673,325
			£ 3,923,097

(The courts might allow a review after 11 years to ERV but taken here through for 14 years)

Tenant's present interest:

ERV		£ 370,000	
Rent reserved		150,000	
Profit rent		£ 220,000	
YP 3 years @ 8%/3% 40p		1.6149	£ 355,278
Reversion		£ 370,000	
Rent reserved (S.34)		260,000	
Profit rent		£ 110,000	
YP 14 yrs @ 8%/3% 40p	7.2188		
PV £ 1 in 3 years @ 8%	.79383	5.7305	£ 630,355
			£ 985,633

(Variable profit rent needs to be checked with more accurate method.)

If the tenant acquires the freehold, the interests would be merged and would be worth:

	£ 370,000
YP perp @ 7%	14.2857
	£ 5,285,709

A freeholder recognising the marriage value will ask for a sum in excess of the open market value of £ 3,923,000.

c) Surrender for new 20 year lease with rent review after 5 years to ERV.
Note: Surrender implies the releasing of all contractual and statutory rights by the tenant. The tenant must therefore account for the fact that in 5 years the rent will be the open-market rental value of the property as demised at the commencement of the new 20 year lease.

Landlord's present interest as b) £3,923,097

Landlord's proposed interest

Let proposed rent for 1st 5 years =	£x	
then	£x	
YP 5 years @ 7%	4.1002	£4.1002x

Reversion to ERV	£370,000	
YP perp def'd 5 years @ 7%	10.1855	£3,768,635
		£3,768,635 + £4.1002x

present = proposed

$$£3,923,097 = £3,768,635 + £4.1002x$$
$$£154,462 = 4.1002x$$
$$£37,671 = x$$

Tenant's view:
Tenant's present interest: £985,633

Tenant's proposed interest

ERV	£370,000	
Rent reserved £x	x	
Profit rent	£370,000-x	
YP 5 years 8%/3% 40p	2.5386	
	£939,282-£2.5386x	

£985,633	=	£939,282-2.5386x
2.5386x	=	£939,282-£985,633
2.5386x	=	-£46.351
x	=	-£18,258

When this occurs in examinations, candidates assume that they have miscalculated. This is not the case; the negative rent is correct. Here a tenant is surrendering very valuable profit rents to be enjoyed over a total of 17 years from today for a new 20 year lease with a profit rent for 5 years. This cannot be achieved unless from the tenant's point of view the landlord pays a reverse rent. Even so the extremes of -£18,258 and +£37,671 are likely to defeat the negotiators. A solution would be for the parties to agree that the rent on review after 5 years will exclude the £110,000 p.a. of tenant's improvements. This emphasises the essential differences between landlords' and tenants' rights under the 1954 Act and the specific provisions of a rent review clause. The two must not be confused.

d) Reposession can only be obtained on the following grounds:
  i) breach of repairing obligation;
  ii) persistent delay or failure to pay rent;
  iii) other substantial breaches of covenants;
  iv) availability of suitable alternative accommodation:
  v) uneconomic sub-letting;
  vi) demolition or substantial reconstruction;
  vii) required by owner for his own occupation (5 year rule).

Solutions

The amount of compensation will vary depending upon grounds, but the maximum would be:

Loss of security under 1954 Act as specified in the 1990 order is 1 or in the case of 14 year occupation it becomes 2 which on £ 350,000 is £ 700,000.

Plus Compensation for Improvements (1927) being the lesser of:
  i) Net addition to value
  ii) Reasonable cost of carrying out the
      improvements at the termination of
      the tenancy

i) Net addition to value		
Rental value improved	£ 370,000	
Unimproved	£ 260,000	
	£ 110,000	
YP perp @ 7%	14.2857	
	£ 1,571,427	
ii) Cost 7 years ago	£ 300,000	
Increase in costs at. say 10% per		
annum x Amount £ for 7 years		
@ 10%	1.9487	
	£ 584,610	

Hence maximum compensation might be £ 700,000 + £ 584,610.

8.1 GDV

$5,000m^2$ (gross) x 85% = $4250m^2$ net

4,250 @ £ 200m^2 p.a.	£ 850,000	
YP perp @ 7%	14.29	£ 12,146,500
Less purchaser's costs and		
stamp duty @ 2.75%		325,089
		£ 11,821,411
Less costs		
a) Building 5,000m^2 @ £ 400m^2	£ 2,000,000	
b) Fees @ 12.5%	250,000	
Total	£ 2,250,000	
c) Finance 14% for 1 year on		
50% of total	157,500	
d) Legal fees (1%) and agents (1%)		
on sale and promotion	276,428	
e) Profit @ 15% GDV	1,773,211	£ 4,457,139
Total costs		£ 7,364,271

Let site value = £ x

Fees on acquisition + stamp duty = 2.5% = 0.025x

Total debt after 1 year @ 15% = 1.025x (1.15)

$$£ 7,364,271 = 1.1787x$$
$$£ 6,247,525 = x$$

Site value = £ 6,247,525 say £ 6,250,000

9.1 a) £1m plus say 4% = £1,040,000
   b) 5.77%

$$\frac{60,000}{1,040,000} \times 100$$

   c) 10.58%

$$\frac{110,000}{1,040,000} \times 100$$

   d) Trial and error try 9½%

Term rent	£60,000	
YP 4 years @ 9½%	3.2045	192.270
Reversion to	£110,000	
YP perp def'd 4 years @ 9½%	7.32183	805,401
		£997,671

Allowing for negotiations on sale price say 9½% i.e. an equivalent yield of 9½% (9.15% on £1,040,000).

   e) Rental growth at 5%

Therefore rent on review =	£110,000
x Amount of £1 for 4 years at 5%	1.2155
	£133,705
Value in 4 years' time at 9½% =	£133,705
	10.5263
	£1,407,421

   Therefore possible cash flow adjusted for growth

0 - £1,040,000		
1	+	£60,000
2	+	£60,000
3	+	£60,000
4	+	£60,000
	+	£1,407,421

IRR by calculator = 13.048%. This yield might be called an equated yield.

   f) Requirement is an IRR or Target rate of 12%

Outlay	=	£1,040,000
Income	=	60,000
		60,000
		60,000
		60,000 + £CV

Term rent	£60,000
YP 4 years at 12%	3.0373
	£182.238

Reversion	x
YP perp at 9½%	
x P.V. £1 in 4 years at 12%	6.6896
	£182.238 + 6.6896x

Solutions

BUT   £ 182,238 + 6,6896x - £ 1,040,000 = NPV = 0.

Therefore   6.6896x =   £ 1,040,000 - £ 182,238

              x =   £ 128,223.21

The rent in Year 4 must have risen to £ 128,223.

Note: For purists the sale disposal costs should be accounted for and Capital Gains Tax if purchased by a taxpayer.

i) £ 18,223

ii) £ 110,000 x

Amount of £ 1 for 4 years at i% = £ 128,223

Amount of £ 1 for 4 years at i% = 128,223 ÷ 110,000

                                         = 1.1656

(1.1656-1) x 100   = 16.56% over 4 years

AND where $(1+i)^4$ = 1.1656

i   = $(\sqrt[4]{1.1656})$ - 1

                                 = 1.0390 - 1

                                 = 0.390 x 100

                                 = 3.9%

9.2   a) IRR = Internal Rate of Return, i.e. the discount rate that makes the Net Present Value of a project equal to zero.

b) The IRR of an investment before allowing for the incidence of taxation.

c) The IRR of a property investment after adjustment for acquisition costs, outgoings but not taxation taking account of current income and reversionary incomes expressed in current value terms.

d) The IRR of a property investment after adjustment for acquisition costs, outgoings but not taxation taking account of current income and reversionary incomes expressed in future value terms.